D1742744

The Truth About ...
Homosexuality
Is It Natural or Not?

By

Frederick K.C. Price, Ph.D.

Faith One Publishing
Los Angeles, California

The Truth About ... Homosexuality
Is It Natural or Not?

ISBN 1-883798-31-0
Copyright ©1999 by
Frederick K.C. Price, Ph.D.
P. O. Box 90000
Los Angeles, CA 90009

Published by Faith One Publishing
7901 South Vermont Avenue
Los Angeles, California 90044

The Truth About ...
Homosexuality

Is It Natural or Not?

The dictionary defines homosexuality as a "condition of or characterized by sexual desire for those of the same sex as oneself." There is no doubt that this condition has existed since man began to multiply and replenish the earth in accordance with Genesis 1:28. Consequently, there are many people today who subscribe to belief that homosexuality is actually a state of birth rather than a state of mind.

In His care and concern for mankind, God has given us guidelines to follow that are essential to success in every area of living. These guidelines are outlined in the Bible — the Word of God. When you look closely at most of our present conditions in society, you see that they are really variations on old themes. This includes the homosexual lifestyle. Let's see what the Bible has to say about this controversial topic, and determine from it how homosexuality measures up in terms of its being normal and acceptable in God's eyes.

Personally, I have no axe to grind, and certainly nothing to gain from taking on the issue of homosexuality. But Jesus Himself said that the truth will make us free (John 8:32), and that is all I am interested in doing — setting people free by teaching them the Word of God and letting them make informed decisions from there.

John 3:16 tells us, **"… God so loved the world that He gave His only begotten Son, that whoever believes in Him should not perish but have everlasting life."** Whoever includes everyone on the face of planet Earth. God loves all mankind so much that He made salvation available to us through His Son in order that we might become His children by accepting Jesus Christ as Savior and Lord. Love, however, also includes being totally honest, whether or not people want to hear what is being said.

Is Homosexuality Natural?

The Apostle Paul writes in Romans 1:21-27:

because, although they knew God, they did not glorify Him as God, nor were thankful, but became futile in their thoughts, and their foolish hearts were darkened.

Professing to be wise, they became fools

and changed the glory of the incorruptible God into an image made like corruptible man — and birds and four-footed animals and creeping things.

Therefore God also gave them up to uncleanness, in the lusts of their hearts, to dishonor their bodies among themselves,

who exchanged the truth of God for the lie, and worshipped and served the creature rather than the Creator, who is blessed forever. Amen.

For this reason God gave them up to vile passions. For even their women exchanged the natural use for what is against nature.

Likewise also the men, leaving the natural use of the woman, burned in their lust for one another, men with men committing what is shameful, and receiving in themselves the penalty of their error which was due.

Notice, in the last two verses, that Paul uses the word *natural*. That is a very interesting and provocative term. The direct opposite of natural, of course, is unnatural — in other words, what is not natural. This indicates that in the sight of God, some things are considered natural, and some are considered unnatural.

For instance, your ears were designed for hearing. They also house the balancing apparatus for the body, so hearing and aiding in balance are natural uses of the ear. You can also use them to hang earrings on, but they were not designed for that purpose, so you could consider wearing earrings to be unnatural. Whether that makes it right or wrong depends on the effect earrings have on your ears.

To my knowledge, there is no case history of a person's hearing being adversely affected by the wearing of earrings. It does not usually cause a problem with the conscience of the wearer. That cannot necessarily be said for unnatural uses of other organs of the body. Some questionable uses can cause damage to the body. Some of them can even put a person into a state of depression, or confusion, or engender a moral crisis that may cause that person to seek professional or spiritual counseling to determine if what he or she is doing is permissible behavior. The unnatural uses that can engender all these negative emotions include homosexual activities, such as anal or oral copulation.

Think about it. What is a penis for? What is a vagina for? What is the anus for? When it comes to sex — or anything else, for that matter — if there is reservation, embarrassment, guilt, or any feelings of unworthiness or of being dirty, chances are that something is out of order.

Every organ of the body has a purpose, and when you violate that purpose, the organ in question can become damaged and not function as efficiently as it should. If you damage your ears and can no longer hear through them, there is no other organ in your body that can perform the same function. Likewise, when you violate your body in other ways, there is a price to pay.

Here is something else to consider. If it were natural for men to be sexually attracted to other men, and women to be sexually attracted to other women, it would be possible for two men or two women to produce a child. This is not the case. Females are the only human beings who can conceive children, and males are the only human beings who can fertilize the eggs of the females. Therefore, homosexuality cannot be natural. It has to be against nature.

Choices and Influences

Some homosexuals and lesbians may think I am being narrow-minded and that I am just another preacher who is down on homosexuality. They may share the opinion one young man had when he wrote me about his homosexuality. In his letter he said, "You do not have any real feeling for us. It is not fair. You should understand us and our lifestyle."

After reading that letter, I asked the Lord to help me understand. After all, I did not invent homosexuality. I did not put the terms *natural* and *against nature* into the Bible. Those expressions were there when I started studying the Word myself many years ago.

Let's read Romans 1:26-27 again, and I will show you what the Holy Spirit revealed to me:

For this reason God gave them up
to vile passions. For even their women

**exchanged the natural use for what is
against nature.**

**Likewise also the men, leaving the
natural use of the woman, burned in
their lust for one another, men with men
committing what is shameful, and receiving in themselves the penalty of their
error which was due.**

Paul says in verse 26, **…For even their
women exchanged the natural use….** He
adds in verse 27, **Likewise** [or in the same
manner] **also the men, leaving the natural use….** The fact that they changed shows
that those men and women were not that
way at birth, and that they had a choice as
to whether or not to change. Otherwise,
they would never have left the natural use
in the first place. The Bible clearly states it

is people who change. No person can blame his homosexuality on the environment, on his parents, or even on the way he was born.

Now, I am the first to admit that our surroundings and other people can influence us. We are all bombarded with outside influences from the time we are children, but we do not have to yield to those influences. Our yielding to them is a matter of choice. A man who is a womanizer is that by choice. He was not born that way. He is an individual who simply lets his body govern him. There have been times in private counseling sessions when women have propositioned me, and my body had been tempted to give into the temptation. I knew it would have been wrong and a sin against God and my wife, and that getting away with it would not make it right, so I resisted that urge.

We all have the capacity to resist temptation. Even Jesus was tempted to sin, and He resisted. Paul writes in Hebrews 4:15, **For we do not have a High Priest who cannot sympathize with our weaknesses, but was in all points tempted as we are, yet without sin.** For Jesus to be tempted, He had to be able to succumb to that temptation. Otherwise, it is not a temptation. If someone offers me a million dollars to get pregnant and have a baby, I can easily say no, because there is no way I can become pregnant. I do not have the physical equipment with which to become pregnant, so it is not a temptation.

According to Paul, Jesus **was in all points tempted as we are.** For that to be true, He had to be tempted with lying, stealing, drugs, alcoholism, fornication, adultery and homosexuality, among other things. He had the ability to give in to all those things, and He did not do so. He was **tempted in all points as we are, yet without sin.** If Jesus was tempted to sin but did not, then that means we, too, do not have to yield when temptation comes to us.

The issue is really not whether or not you have a desire to do something, or that you are tempted to do it. The real issue is what you do with that desire. You can choose whether or not to yield to that temptation, just as I had the opportunity to choose whether or not to break my marriage vows and offend God.

Consider the same principle with regard to homosexuality. It says in Romans

1:26 and 27 that the people chose to follow unnatural desires. That also means a person can choose to resist an unnatural desire. That person can control the urge to sin. The urge should not control the person. A man's physical attraction to another man or a woman's attraction to another woman is not justification to act upon that urge.

When You Yield

In case a person still wants to yield to those urges, Paul tells us this in Romans 1:28:

> **And even as they did not like to retain God in their knowledge, God gave them over to a debased mind, to do those things which are not fitting.**

According to this verse, the person with a debased mind is hindered when it comes to making sound decisions. And in life you have to make decisions: I will do this, I will not do that. If you do not make sound judgments, you stand a good chance of doing some or all of **those things which are not fitting** listed in Romans 1:29-31:

Being filled with all unright-eousness, sexual immorality, wicked-ness, covetousness, maliciousness; full of envy, murder, strife, deceit, evil-mindedness; they are whisperers,

backbiters, haters of God, violent, proud, boasters, inventors of evil things, disobedient to parents,

undiscerning, untrustworthy, un-loving, unforgiving, unmerciful.

Paul adds in verse 32:

> **who, knowing the righteous judg-
> ment of God, that those who practice
> such things are deserving of death, not
> only do the same but also approve of
> those who practice them.**

When you do something that is bla-
tantly wrong, you generally know it is
wrong at the time you do it, and you have
something nagging at you from the inside,
bugging you about it. Many people call
these promptings "unctions" or "conscience," but in reality, they are the voice
of your human spirit.

According to the Bible, man is a tri-
partite being (1 Thessalonians 5:23). He
(or she) is a spirit, with a soul, existing in

a physical body. God deals with man through his spirit, because God Himself is a Spirit (John 4:24). With his soul (his intellect, will and emotions) man is able to deal in the mental realm; with his body, he is able to contact the physical realm through his five senses of touch, sight, sound, taste, and smell.

An unsaved man is still a spirit, as well as the saved man. He, too, has a soul and he lives inside a physical body. The only difference between an unsaved individual and a Christian is that the unsaved person has not made Jesus Christ his personal Savior and Lord, and is thereby not able to be called a child of God.

However, your spirit, whether saved or unsaved, has no more power to make you do right or to do wrong than the traffic signal on a corner has the ability to make you stop. You can very easily drive through an intersection when the signal advises you to stop, and you may hit another car or a pedestrian when you do so, but that is not the signal's fault. The responsibility lies solely with you.

It is also possible to "sear" your conscience (the voice of your spirit) or to harden your heart (the spirit and heart are the same), so that you do not hear what your spirit/heart is saying any more. In other words, the searing of your conscience can be compared to a steak that has been seared on the outside to seal the meat's juices in. Your conscience can become so seared that very little can get in to affect it.

Here is something else to consider in verse 32:

Who knowing the righteous judgment of God, that those who practice such things are deserving of death….

Paul does not say that God will kill you for doing those things. God has nothing to do with murder, sickness, disease, or anything else that can wipe you out. He is not the author of AIDS or any other sexually transmitted disease. All God wants to do is to forgive us and take care of us as His children. That is why He made salvation available to mankind through Christ. However, our continuing to act on "those things which are not fitting" will open the door for the negative things such as murder, sickness, and disease to come into our lives. That is what God means when He says through Paul **that those who practice such things are deserving of death.**

God does not want you to die, but He will allow death to take you, just as He allows you to do the things that can eventually kill you. God gave you a free will, and He will not violate that will. However, He wants to let you know what can happen so you will be informed and make right judgments. You are responsible for the decisions you make, and the consequences that arise from them. God will allow you to succumb to destruction, such as AIDS and other negative things associated with sin, but it is not His choice. It is yours.

What Paul says in Romans 1:32 is not limited to sinners only. Christians are just as subject to Paul's admonition as sinners are. Some Christians fornicate and commit adultery, act maliciously and enviously, gossip and do everything else listed in Romans 1:29-31. And these sins cause them problems, just as they do sinners, including sickness and disease. However, Christians are still saved, because Jesus has already paid the price on the cross at Calvary to set them free. They are just unable to claim the total salvation package for living a successful Christian lifestyle, which includes prosperity, divine healing, peace, and joy in the Lord, along with eternal life.

Sure, Sin Can Be Fun, But …

Some people enjoy the homosexual and lesbian lifestyle. But because there may be pleasure in participating in that kind of lifestyle does not make it right. In fact,

Proverbs 9:17-18 tells us, **"Stolen water is sweet, and bread eaten in secret is pleasant." But he does not know that the dead are there; that her guests are in the depths of hell.** That is extremely similar to what we read in Romans 1:32, about the people who act on these things being deserving of death.

You may engage in homosexuality because you feel it is part of your inborn nature. That is the devil (the cause of sin in the world) feeding false thoughts to your mind. I want to reiterate this fact because it is so important, that people are not born with homosexual desires, but they can be that way if they choose. Perhaps, deep down inside, you know it is not right. But because it seems as if more and more people are falling into this lifestyle than say 10 or 15 years ago, you may think it must be all right. It is not!

According to the Bible, homosexuality is as much a sin as murder, lying or stealing. Sin is sin, hell is hell, and the lake of fire is the lake of fire. God says in Romans 6:23 that the wages of sin is death.

Personally, I do not think any worse of the homosexual than I do of the adulterer, fornicator, liar, or thief. And from what I have gathered from my study of the Bible, neither does God. He loves the sinner, and wants that person to turn his or her life over to Jesus.

If there is something in your past or your personality you cannot deal with alone, you can come to the Lord Jesus Christ, and by the power of God through

His Holy Spirit, He will help you. If you truly want to be free, Jesus is the answer. Whether or not you accept that as your answer is entirely up to you.

Prayer For Salvation

If you are not a Christian and would like to accept Jesus as the answer to your life, I would like you to pray the following prayer:

Dear God:

Thank you for sending Your Son Jesus Christ to destroy the spiritual and the physical power of death over my life. I accept Jesus now as my personal Savior and Lord, and choose life by turning away from the sins of my past to a renewed life in Jesus.

You said that if I would confess with my mouth the Lord Jesus and believe in my heart that You raised Him from the dead, then I would be saved. I do that now. I believe Jesus died for my sin and that You raised Him from the dead for my benefit. So, I thank You for the gift of salvation and I thank You for accepting me now as Your child. In Jesus' name, Amen.

Parts of this mini-book are taken from two larger bodies of teaching entitled

Beware! The Lies of Satan
and
Homosexuality: State of Birth or State of Mind?

by the same author.

Copies of these books are available at local bookstores

or by calling (800) 943-4388

For more information, please write:

Crenshaw Christian Center
P.O. Box 90000
Los Angeles CA 90009

Or check your local TV listing for:

The Ever Increasing Faith
Television Program

Or check out our WebSite at:

www.faithdome.org

About the Author

Frederick K. C. Price, Ph.D., founded Crenshaw Christian Center in Los Angeles, California, in 1973, with a congregation of some 300 people. Today, the church's membership numbers well over 18,000 members of various racial backgrounds.

Crenshaw Christian Center, home of the renowned 10,146-seat FaithDome, has a staff of more than 300 employees. Included on its 30-acre grounds are a Ministry Training Institute, the Frederick K.C. Price III elementary and junior and senior high schools, as well as the FKCP III Preschool.

The *Ever Increasing Faith* television and radio broadcasts are outreaches of Crenshaw Christian Center. The television program is viewed on more than 100 stations worldwide. The radio program airs on over 40 stations across the country and internationally.

Dr. Price travels extensively, teaching on the Word of Faith simply and understandably in the power of the Holy Spirit. He is the author of several books on faith, divine healing, prosperity, and the Holy Spirit.

In 1990, Dr. Price founded the Fellowship of Inner-City Word of Faith Ministries (FICWFM) for the purpose of fostering and spreading the faith message among independent ministries located in the metropolitan areas of the United States.

❏ YES, I would like information on:

    ❏ Other books and materials by
        Dr. Frederick K.C. Price.

    ❏ Dr. Price's Ever Increasing Faith
        Television & Radio Program.

    ❏ Add me to your mailing list
        to receive information on
        your new publications
        and materials.

Name: _____

Address: _____

City: _____

State: _____ Zip Code: _____

NO POSTAGE
NECESSARY
IF MAILED
IN THE
UNITED STATES

If you would like to help save us
postage, please place a stamp here

BUSINESS REPLY MAIL

FIRST CLASS MAIL   PERMIT NO 65731   LOS ANGELES CA 90009

POSTAGE WILL BE PAID BY ADDRESSEE

EIF Ministries / Faith One Publishing
P.O. Box 90000
Los Angeles CA 90099-2849